ANIMAL KINGDOM

180°

Nicholas Blechman

INTRODUCTION

From the great blue whale to the tiniest insect (and of course, to us, humankind), we are all connected by the tree of life, having evolved over millions of years from tiny basic organisms that lived on Earth more than 3.4 billion years ago.

The number of animals that can be found today has exploded to more than 1.9 million species, and scientists are still making thousands of new discoveries each year. With many of these undiscovered species hidden in the depths of rainforests that are now under threat from mankind, some may become extinct before we even knew they existed.

Every single one of these animals has found its own unique place in nature and has adapted to survive in its particular environment, developing its shape, colour, way of reproducing, diet, and abilities through the process of evolution.

This book introduces you to extraordinary animals from around the world and some of the best facts and figures to be found in nature, brought to life by incredible infographics. So turn the page to understand the facts in the blink of an eye.

SPECIES

The animal kingdom is made up of an amazing array of different creatures.

Animals are set apart from plants by their ability to move freely, the presence of a central nervous system, and their need to consume other living organisms to survive.

There are two main types of animal: vertebrates, which have a backbone, and invertebrates, which do not. The vertebrate and invertebrate families can be divided into smaller groups, like reptiles, birds and mammals, that are made up of different species that share similar features.

Different species have developed unique characteristics over billions of years through evolution, meaning that all the hugely varied animals share a common starting point from many billions of years ago.

While most of this book showcases the abilities of individual species, here is a look at how animals have developed into different groups, and why...

ORIGIN OF SPECIES

Charles Darwin studied animals to learn more about evolution. He spent his life looking at the differences between the amazing variety of species on Earth.

Darwin spotted that different animal species had unique adaptations that made them perfectly suited to their particular environment. For instance, birds' beaks are shaped differently depending on what they eat.

 Eats seeds

 Eats insects

 Eats fruit

WIN THE DAY

In nature, every species wants to pass on its genes by producing offspring. However, in the wild, many animals die before they reach full maturity – the time when they can mate and reproduce. With so many animals on Earth, there is a lot of competition to survive.

NATURAL SELECTION

Being able to endure tougher conditions, being faster at finding food, or being better at hiding from predators could all improve an animal's chances of surviving into maturity. These superior characteristics will also catch the eye of a mate, who will want to pass them on to its young. This process is known as natural selection.

ONE AND ONLY

Darwin realised that over thousands of years, animals' characteristics had become refined, making each species uniquely adapted to its environment.

This book is packed with animals that possess some striking features. Here are some of the reasons why they have developed these unique adaptations.

FAST AND FURIOUS

Having supreme speed and strength are useful for catching dinner.

SELF-DEFENCE

Having good armour reduces an animal's risk of becoming somebody else's meal.

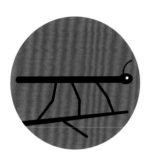

UNDER COVER

A well-camouflaged animal is less likely to be spotted by a predator.

LEG UP

A physical advantage that provides greater access to food lessens the risk of starvation.

SHOW-OFF

Being more attractive to a mate increases an animal's chances of passing on its genes.

STRETCH YOUR LEGS

Humans have their own evolution story, developing from early primates into the walking, talking, deep-thinking species that we are today.

11

CLASS OF
THEIR OWN

The animal kingdom is made
up from millions of different species
of animals. These species can
be sorted into different groups,
each of which has developed a similar
set of characteristics.

WARM-BLOODED ANIMALS
regulate the temperature
of their bodies.

IN FINE FEATHER
Birds are warm-blooded
vertebrates.

They breathe
with lungs.

They have beaks.

They have a
pair of wings.

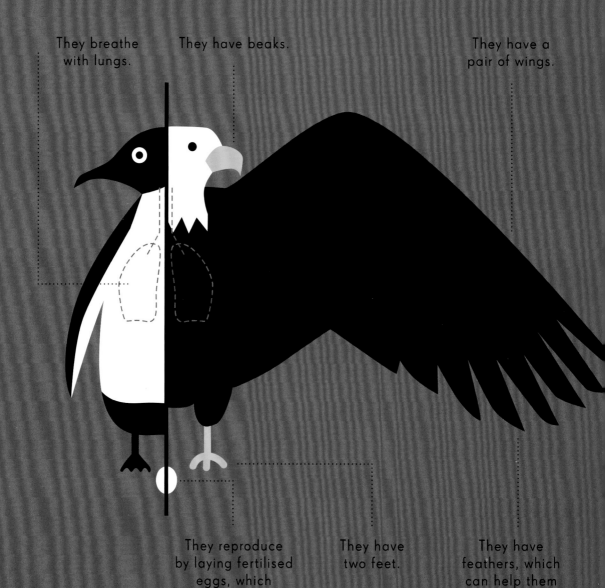

They reproduce
by laying fertilised
eggs, which
they primarily
hatch in nests.

They have
two feet.

They have
feathers, which
can help them
to fly or swim.

FUR COAT
Mammals are warm-blooded vertebrates.

Most **mammals** have fur or hair to protect their skin.

The females give birth to live young and produce milk to nourish them.

Mammals are suited to living either on land or in the water.

They breathe with their lungs — meaning that dolphins and other mammals that live in the water need to hold their breath and come up for air.

Most have four limbs in the form of arms, legs, flippers or wings.

Most have a tail in addition to their other limbs.

HAVE SOME BACKBONE
Vertebrates have backbones and a complex brain, making them the most advanced organisms on the planet.

Although **vertebrates** only make up 3% of the animal kingdom, there are around 62,000 different species – the most intelligent of which is you, a human being!

BLOOD RUNNING COLD

Cold-blooded animals take on the temperature of their surroundings. Many need to bask in the sun in order to keep their body temperature up.

TWIN FINS
Fish are vertebrates suited to living underwater. Most are cold-blooded.

Most **fish** are covered in waterproof scales.

Most reproduce by laying unfertilised eggs.

They breathe underwater with pairs of gills.

They have fins and a tail help them to swim.

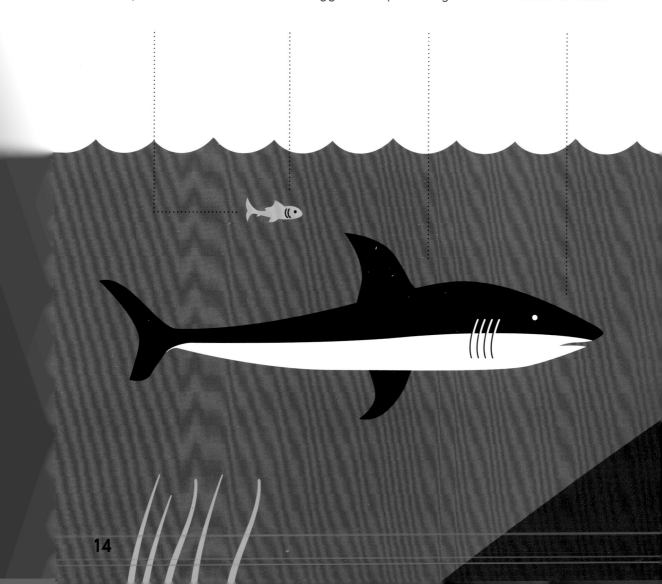

LIFE AQUATIC

Amphibians are cold-blooded vertebrates.

They can live in water or on land.

Most have small lungs, but also breathe through their skin.

They reproduce by laying eggs in water. These eggs hatch into aquatic larvae.

Most have four limbs.

SCALED BACK

Reptiles are also cold-blooded vertebrates.

They can live in water or on land.

They breathe with lungs.

Almost all reproduce by laying fertilised soft-shelled eggs on land.

Most have four limbs, but some – like snakes – have none.

Reptiles bask in the sun for warmth.

They are covered in hard scales.

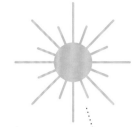

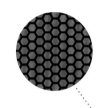

TOTALLY SPINELESS

Invertebrates have no backbone, although most of them can move. Some – like coral – look like plants, but they have no cell walls and cannot make their own food for energy, so are classified as animals.

SPONGE BATH
Although they don't have organs, such as lungs or a heart, **Porifera** are still classed as animals. They live in the water and feed on small organisms.

SHELL SUIT
Molluscs, such as clams or snails, are suited to living either on land or in the water. Most have shells, soft bodies, and no legs at all.

NASTY STING
Cnidarians, such as jellyfish, live in the water and are armed with stinging cells to ward off predators. Their bodies are either wheel or tube-shaped.

FLAT PACK
Platyhelminths are flatworms with soft, segmented bodies. Half of these species are parasitic, stealing nutrients from their host animal, causing disease.

16

ROUND THE TWIST
Nematodes are tiny roundworms. Some, such as hookworm or Loa loa, can cause disease in humans.

SUPER STAR
Echinoderms have thousands of tiny feet on their arms, and can regrow a broken limb. They live in salt water.

NO LEG TO STAND ON
Annelids are segmented worms with no legs, and can be found in water or on land.

SINGLE CELL
Whilst they aren't strictly animals, **protozoa** (tiny single cell organisms) are called 'animal-like' because they feed on other organisms and move.

POD SQUAD
Three-quarters of the creatures in the world are **arthropods**, including crabs, insects and spiders. They have segmented bodies and six or more legs.

SENSES

Animals rely on their senses to make smart choices, using them to locate food without wasting energy, to find a mate, and stay safe when it matters most.

Avoiding predators or finding prey isn't just about strength and speed — often it's about spotting an attacker coming or outwitting a target with superior senses.

Some animals have senses that are similar to those of humans, but much more precise. Others have adapted to explore the world using senses that seem strange and different from our own, such as echolocation, night vision and ultrasound, which are useful when an animal is finding its way in the dark or living underwater.

Sometimes an animal's reliance on a particular sense has led to the species developing a feature in a certain way. Find out in this chapter who has a star-shaped nose and which animal has eyes the size of dinner plates!

SEEING

Whether an animal is out to catch prey, or trying to avoid its enemies, a good sense of sight is vital. But different needs and different habitats have caused animals' eyesight to develop in different ways...

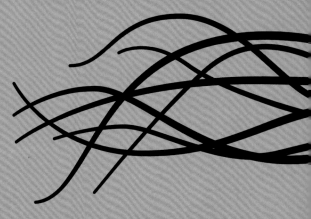

GOT IT COVERED

Dragonflies have huge eyes that almost cover their whole heads. These are made up of 30,000 optical units called ommatidia. They can see colours that humans can't such as ultraviolet (UV) light.

ALL-SEEING

Chameleons' eyes can move and focus independently, which gives them 360-degree vision.

BLIND SPOT

Rhinoceroses have terrible eyesight and cannot see a person standing still if they are more than 30 metres/ 100 feet away. With eyes on opposite sides of their heads, they have to look with one eye at a time to see straight ahead.

UNDER ITS SKIN

Mole rats live in complete darkness underground and rely on their other senses to survive. Their small eyes have evolved to be covered entirely by skin, which makes them truly blind.

WIDE-EYED

Tarsiers have the largest eye-to-body ratio of any mammal. If a human's eyes were proportionally as big, they would be the size of grapefruits! This makes their heads heavy, so they wait silently to catch their prey.

Their eyes are fixed in their skulls and can't turn in their sockets. Instead, **tarsiers** use their flexible necks to rotate their heads 180 degrees.

OPEN WIDE

With wide-set eyes, an **eagle's** field of vision is much wider than a human's...

allowing the **eagle** to clearly see an object at 6 metres/20 feet that a **human** could only see with the same precision at 1.5 metres/5 feet away.

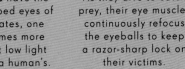

LOOK FORWARD

Forward-facing eyes and stereoscopic vision allow **tawny owls** to work out depth and solidity.

Tawny owls have the best developed eyes of all vertebrates, one hundred times more sensitive at low light levels than a human's.

BIRD'S EYE VIEW

Eagles can spot prey from 2 miles/ 3.2 kilometres away.

As they dive to catch prey, their eye muscles continuously refocus the eyeballs to keep a razor-sharp lock on their victims.

GOOD LOOKING

Hammerhead sharks have unbeatable all-round vision. The location of their eyes gives them a 360-degree look at the world.

360°

BROUGHT TO LIGHT

Colossal squid live about 1,000 metres/3,280 feet under the sea.

With the biggest eyes in the animal world (30 centimetres/11.8 inches) and light organs (called photophores) acting like headlights, they can see in the dim light of the deep ocean.

MONOCULAR VISION

Most animals that are hunted have monocular vision, with eyes on either side of their heads to keep them alert to predators. Whilst able to see an object in the distance, they cannot tell exactly how far away the object is.

BINOCULAR VISION

Most carnivorous mammals and all birds of prey have binocular vision, with two eyes that both face forward. Binocular vision allows predators to hone in on prey, quickly and accurately determining striking distance.

HEARING

Animals have developed their hearing to be able to do some astonishing things. They use their heightened sense of hearing to hunt, communicate and find their way about.

NIGHT OWL

Tawny owls hunt at night in total darkness. They can figure out in 0.01 seconds the exact direction of a scurrying mouse.

This is thanks to large earholes located at slightly different levels, giving them directional hearing, which lets them work out exactly where a sound is coming from.

A tawny owl's hearing is ten times better than a human's.

NO LOVE LOST

Elephants have great hearing, which they need to be able to communicate over distances more than 1 mile/1.6 kilometres.

This is important when a female wants to let males know that she is ready to mate, which only happens every four to five years.

They use infrasonic sounds, which are too deep for a human ear to hear.

HUNT HIGH AND LOW

Cats have 32 muscles in their ears, allowing them to rotate each one independently up to 180 degrees. This lets them pick up sounds and work out where they are coming from.

A cat can detect higher-pitched sounds than humans can, making them able to hear the noises small rodents might make.

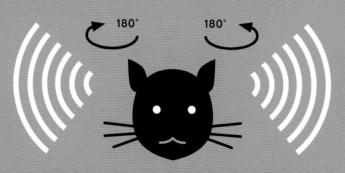

HOME STRAIGHT

Homing pigeons can fly back thousands of miles to reach home from places they have never even been to before.

Scientists think that particles of iron in a pigeon's beak act like a compass, aligning north with the Earth's magnetic field and helping the bird to navigate its way home.

In the past, this ability made a pigeon useful in carrying messages over long distances quickly – it would fly home with a thin scroll of paper attached to its leg.

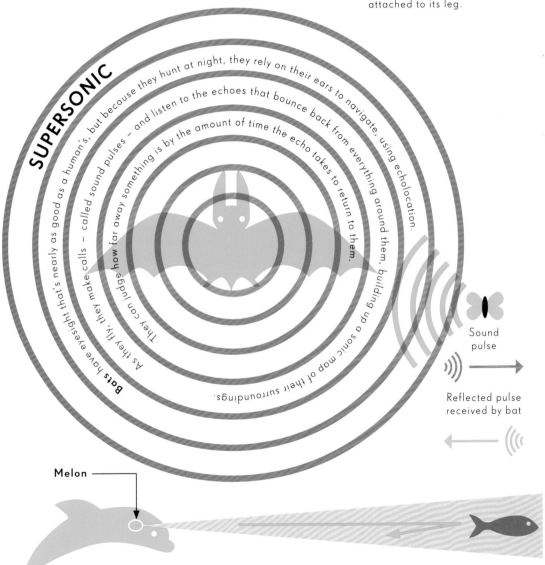

SUPERSONIC

Bats have eyesight that's nearly as good as a human's, but because they hunt at night, they rely on their ears to navigate, using echolocation. As they fly, they make calls – called sound pulses – and listen to the echoes that bounce back from everything around them, building up a sonic map of their surroundings. They can judge how far away something is by the amount of time the echo takes to return to them.

Sound pulse

Reflected pulse received by bat

Melon

SOUNDING OUT

A **dolphin** hunts using a similar technique to that of bats, letting out high-pitched clicks from an organ inside its head called a melon. The dolphin listens out for an echo returning from any fish in its path to pinpoint the fish's whereabouts.

BEING NOSEY

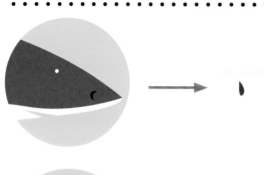

REMARKABLE SHARKS
Sharks can smell chemicals that fish give out to warn one another of danger and can detect blood from over 1 mile/1.6 kilometres away.

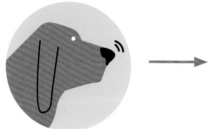

ON THE SCENT
The surface area dedicated to sensing smell is 76 times bigger in a **bloodhound** than it is in a human, with four billion olfactory nerves (for smelling), compared to the 12 million a human has.

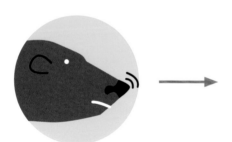

LED BY THE NOSE
The **silvertip grizzly bear** has an even more acute sense of smell – seven times better than a bloodhound! It can smell prey up to 18 miles/ 29 kilometres away, and can detect its presence for up to 48 hours after the animal has left the scene.

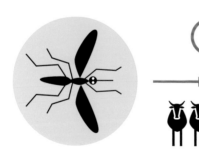

IN THE BULL PEN
Mosquitoes have a sense of smell 10,000 times better than a human's. When we breathe, we let out carbon dioxide and lactic acid that mosquitoes can detect, making them able to search out a human in a field full of cows.

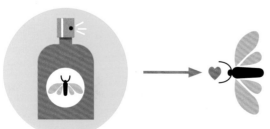

LOVE IN THE AIR
To attract a mate, female **moths** let out a chemical scent. Male moths can smell this up to 30 miles/48 kilometres away with their antennae, 70% of which are dedicated to detecting this scent alone.

TOUCHY SUBJECT

Animals have developed a sense of touch to be able to do things that humans cannot, helping them to survive in the wild.

LUCKY STARS

A **star-nosed mole** has 22 tentacles, containing more than 25,000 receptive organs in a space smaller than 1 square centimetre/ 0.16 square inch.

These tentacles are very sensitive to touch and to electrical impulses, allowing them to find prey without needing any sense of sight at all.

GOOD VIBRATIONS

Crocodiles have thousands of tiny receptors around their jaws that let them sense the vibrations of prey in the water, helping them to detect and locate their victims.

BY A WHISKER

Catfish have an enhanced sense of touch. Instead of scales, they have smooth skin covered with fine hairs, or whiskers, through which they feel.

SEALED FATE

Seals use their whiskers to seek out the fattest fish and track them up to 180 metres/591 feet away. They have more nerve fibres in their whiskers than any other creature.

25

RECORD BREAKERS

The world is full of creatures that achieve the unimaginable every day, having developed enhanced abilities to ensure their own survival. Whether it's due to their strength, speed or sheer size, each sector of the animal kingdom has its own set of record breakers.

To avoid becoming somebody else's lunch, some seek safety in numbers and swarm together in tightly packed clusters to confuse their predators. Others have learned to defend themselves by launching something off-putting at their attackers.

Hunters, like the cheetah, sprint at incredible speeds to capture their prey. Grazers, on the other hand, can travel thousands of miles around the globe just to find the best feeding grounds or to raise their young.

Extraordinary, diverse and sometimes strange, here is a rundown of some of the animal kingdom's most astounding record breakers...

GROUND HERO

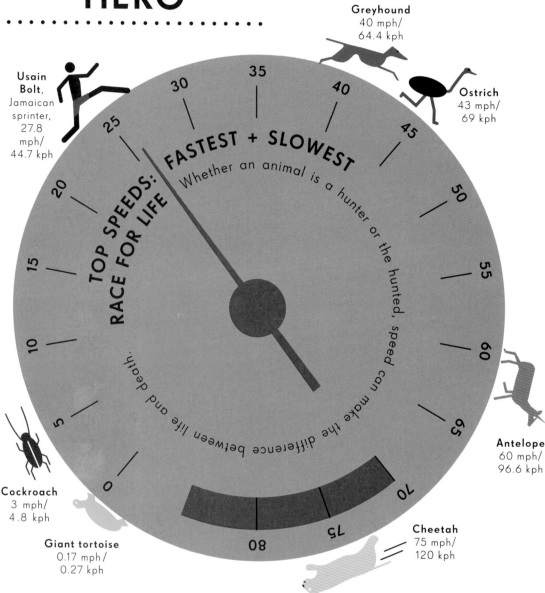

Greyhound
40 mph/
64.4 kph

Usain Bolt, Jamaican sprinter, 27.8 mph/ 44.7 kph

Ostrich
43 mph/
69 kph

TOP SPEEDS: RACE FOR LIFE

FASTEST + SLOWEST

Whether an animal is a hunter or the hunted, speed can make the difference between life and death.

30 35 40 45 50 25 55 20 60 15 65 10 70 5 75 0 08

Cockroach
3 mph/
4.8 kph

Giant tortoise
0.17 mph/
0.27 kph

Antelope
60 mph/
96.6 kph

Cheetah
75 mph/
120 kph

CHAMPION THROWERS

Termites can fire a sticky fluid from their heads.

Pistol shrimps can emit enormously powerful streams of bubbles.

Camels can projectile vomit towards a threat.

WEIGHT LIFTERS

Being strong is all relative – while an elephant is renowned for its strength, it is by no means the most impressive weightlifter. Look at this selection of animals to see which can bear the most in comparison to its own body weight.

Rhinoceros beetle:
85,000%

Leafcutter ant:
5,000%

Bald eagle:
400%

Tiger:
200%

Elephant:
160%

SUPER SWIMMERS

SAVE YOUR BREATH
Some animals that live in the water don't have gills, so they have to hold their breath as they swim. But who can last the longest underwater?

Harbour seal
5 minutes

Dolphin
8 minutes

Walrus
10 minutes

Human
22 minutes*

Northern elephant seal
30 minutes

Alligator
2 hours

PACKED LIKE SARDINES
The **sardine** run is one of the biggest coordinated shoaling movements of fish. They spawn near the African coast. The shoals can be up to 4.5 miles/ 7 kilometres long, 1 mile/1.6 kilometres wide and are visible from space.

The shoaling fish respond to the position of their neighbours, trying not to get too close to some and keeping far enough away from others.

At 12.5 metres/41 feet, the **whale shark** is the longest fish in the world.

THE SQUID AND THE WHALE SHARK
A **giant squid** reaches up to 18 metres/59 feet long.

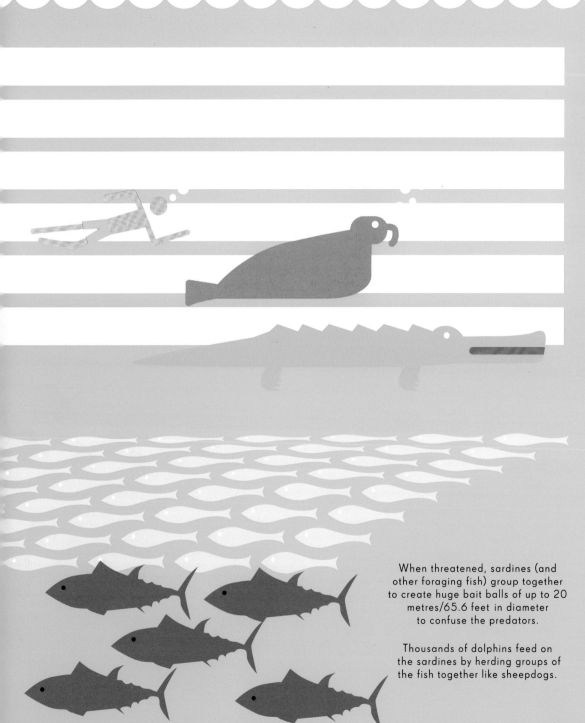

* This is the longest time ever recorded for a human being. The average time a human can hold their breath is only around 1 minute.

When threatened, sardines (and other foraging fish) group together to create huge bait balls of up to 20 metres/65.6 feet in diameter to confuse the predators.

Thousands of dolphins feed on the sardines by herding groups of the fish together like sheepdogs.

TOP FLIGHT

FAST AND FURIOUS

Peregrine falcons have a top speed of 242 mph/390 kph, making them the fastest living beings on Earth.

SAFETY IN NUMBERS

Many birds flock to defend against predators, forming huge crowds. Here are some of the most impressive flocks to be found on Earth.

Red-billed quelea: 1,000,000

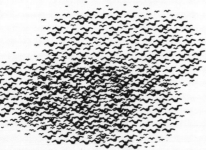

Starling: 250,000

Lapwing: 400

LIGHT AS A FEATHER?

A **pigeon's** feathers weigh more than its bones.

MAKING MOUNTAINS

Fifty **Canada geese** can produce 2.25 metric tons/ 2.5 tons of excrement, or poop, in a year.

STANDING TALL

At 1.2 metres/ 4 feet, the flightless **Greater Rhea** is the tallest bird in South America.

ON THE FLY

Some species of bird make long journeys each year to find the best conditions for breeding, and to avoid harsh winters. But which birds have the most impressive migration routes?

Sooty shearwater **Arctic tern** **Pied wheatear**

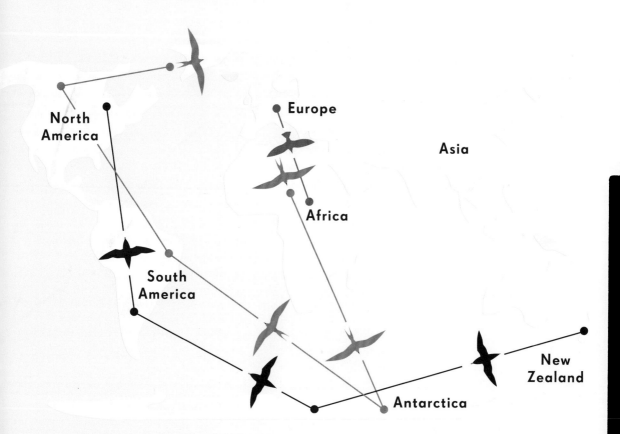

North America

Europe

Asia

Africa

South America

New Zealand

Antarctica

LOST YOUR VOICE?

Only a few species of birds have no voice: storks, pelicans and some **vultures**.

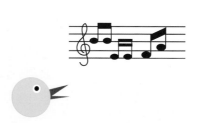

ON SONG

Birdsong can tell you how healthy a bird is – the more complex the song, the healthier the bird.

BIG THINKERS

The size of an animal's brain, compared to its body, can give a basic idea as to its intelligence. This means that a cat (ratio 1:110) is much cleverer than a hippopotamus (ratio 1:2789).

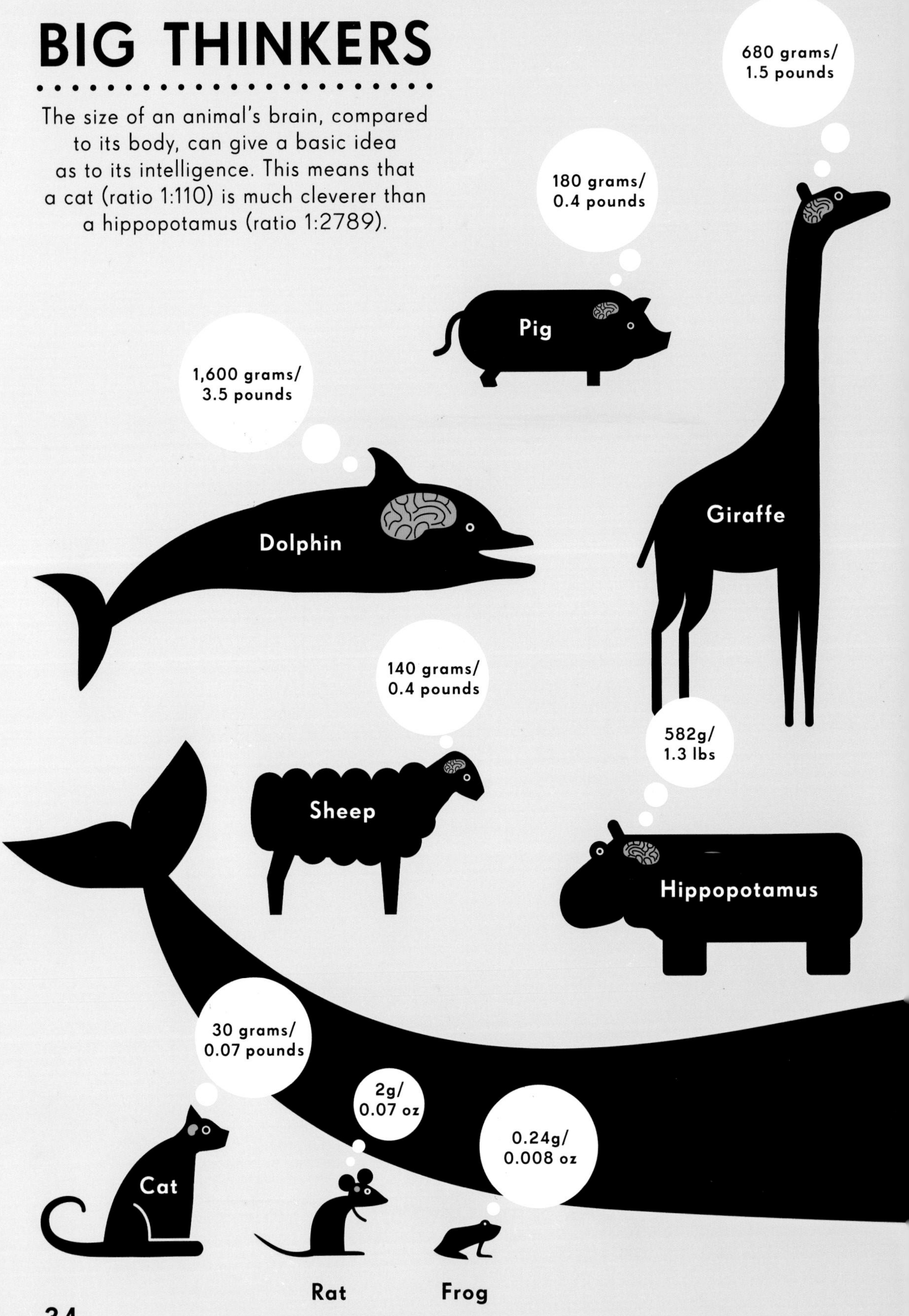

680 grams/
1.5 pounds

180 grams/
0.4 pounds

Pig

Giraffe

1,600 grams/
3.5 pounds

Dolphin

140 grams/
0.4 pounds

582g/
1.3 lbs

Sheep

Hippopotamus

30 grams/
0.07 pounds

2g/
0.07 oz

0.24g/
0.008 oz

Cat

Rat

Frog

Monkey

1,400 grams/
3 pounds

BRIGHT SPARKS

Size isn't everything, though, when it comes to intelligence. Humans have more cortical neurons (the nerve cells that make up the cortex of the brain), which puts us at the top of the intelligence rankings.

375g/
0.83 lbs

4,783 grams/
10.5 pounds

22 grams/
0.05 pounds

Adult

Newborn

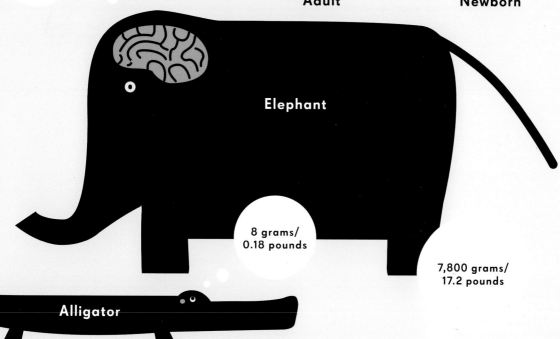

Elephant

8 grams/
0.18 pounds

7,800 grams/
17.2 pounds

Alligator

Sperm whale

FOOD AND DRINK

All animals need food and drink to live. But what they consume, how much and how often, can vary wildly.

What an animal eats determines where it sits in the food chain, with predators at the top and their prey beneath them. It also affects the shape and number of their teeth, the length of their tongues and size of their mouths.

Most animals don't follow a regular eating pattern of three meals a day. While some, like the kingfisher, eat more than half their body weight in a day, others, like the blue whale, can go for eight months of the year without eating at all!

Here is a look at what some of nature's most interesting beasties have on their menu, and how to tell a plant-eating herbivore from a meat-eating carnivore. You never know, it might come in useful one day!

FOOD CHAIN

The food chain is a continuous process. At any moment something
is being eaten, dies, breaks down, and is being eaten again.
It can never have less than three stages.

Here's how it can work:

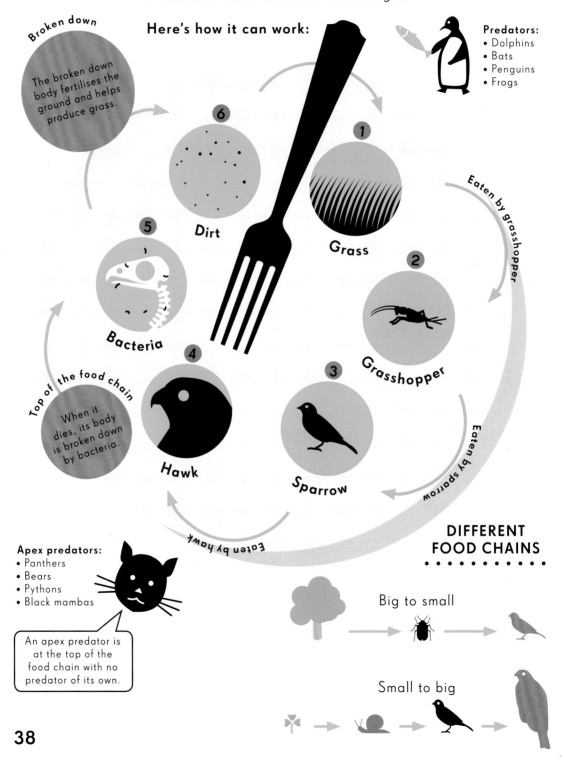

Broken down

The broken down body fertilises the ground and helps produce grass.

Predators:
• Dolphins
• Bats
• Penguins
• Frogs

6 Dirt

1 Grass

Eaten by grasshopper

5 Bacteria

2 Grasshopper

Top of the food chain

When it dies, its body is broken down by bacteria.

Eaten by sparrow

4 Hawk

3 Sparrow

Eaten by hawk

Apex predators:
• Panthers
• Bears
• Pythons
• Black mambas

An apex predator is at the top of the food chain with no predator of its own.

DIFFERENT FOOD CHAINS

Big to small

Small to big

WHALE-SIZE LUNCH

The largest animal on Earth has a food chain with only three links. (No other mammal on the planet is two steps above microscopic in the food chain.)

A **blue whale** may consume up to 6.3 – 7.3 metric tons/6.9 – 8 tons of food per day during the summer feeding season.

That's 3,628 kilograms/8,000 pounds of krill per day!

For the other eight months of the year, it apparently doesn't eat anything at all, living off stored fat.

Jan	Feb	Mar	Apr	May	Jun	Jul	Aug	Sep	Oct	Nov	Dec

Eats   **Does not eat**

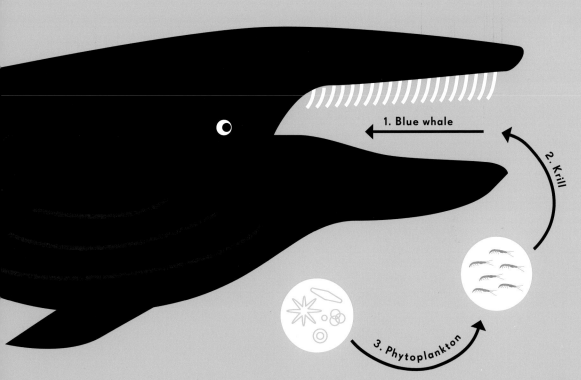

1. Blue whale

2. Krill

3. Phytoplankton

39

CARNIVORES

Carnivores eat a diet based on meat.

Sweat is released through their tongues, as many carnivores hunt at night and therefore don't need to sweat through their skin to stay cool.

Eyes tend to face forwards to allow proper depth perception for hunting.

Jaws move up and down but not side to side.

Teeth are sharp, long and pointed. They are built to tear prey apart.

Saliva contains no digestive enzymes.

Tongue laps up water. Cats can't taste sweet flavours (although dogs can).

FISH FOOD

Piranhas are thought of as carnivorous fish, when in fact they are omnivorous, often eating plants as well as meat.

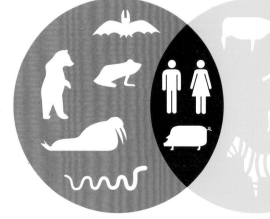

Omnivores

Herbivores

Carnivores

HERBIVORES

Herbivores eat a diet based on plants.

Sweat is released through their skin, as herbivore animals tend to gather food during the day.

Eyes are often on the side of the head, to spot danger from behind.

Jaws move up and down and side to side.

Teeth are flat with squared back molars to grind food.

Saliva is alkaline, containing carbohydrate digestive enzymes to predigest or break down plant food.

Tongue can taste sweet things. Mouths are used to suck up water.

THINK CARNIVORES ARE THE ONES TO LOOK OUT FOR? THINK AGAIN.

Cape buffaloes are short-tempered South African herbivores, who will charge at attackers such as lions.

Wild boar weigh up to 181 kg/400 lbs and some have sharp tusks.

Hippopotamuses kill more humans than lions, leopards or crocodiles.

Male elephants have hormone surges that make them violent.

HELP!

41

OPEN WIDE

BIG MOUTH

A **hippo** can extend its mouth to 180 degrees.

TONGUE TWISTER

5 centimetres/2 inches

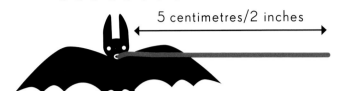

The **tube-lipped nectar bat** has the longest tongue of any known mammal, compared to its body length.

TONGUE-TIED

The **giraffe** can extend its tongue 45 centimetres/18 inches.

SENSE OF DIRECTION

The **snake**'s forked tongue acts as a directional detector that can find other animals in their local environment.

LICKETY SPIT

A **chameleon**'s tongue travels at 400 metres/1,312 feet per second, about 41 Gs of force. A space shuttle only develops about 3G of force when it takes off.

TWO TON TONGUE

A **blue whale**'s tongue weighs 2.7 metric tons/3 tons.

GRIN AND BEAR IT

How do animals compare when you count the number of teeth they have?

Rat: 16

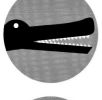

Rabbit: 28

Human: 32

Crocodile: 70

Burmese python: 100

Dolphin: 252

WHAT A MOUTHFUL

How many types of bacteria are there in the mouths of different animals?

Human's mouth

615

Dog's mouth

600

Mouse's mouth

200

BIG BELLIES

How much do different animals eat compared to the size of their bodies?

Duck:
20%

Mouse:
15%

Chicken:
7.5%

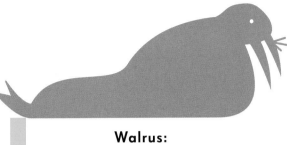

Walrus:
6%

Cow:
2.5%

THIRSTY WORK

How much water do different animals consume in a day?

Budgie: 2 millilitres per day

Turkey: 470 millilitres per day

Sow pig: 17,000 millilitres per day

Polar bear: 23,000 millilitres per day

Northern elephant seal: 54,000 millilitres per day

EAT LIKE
A BIRD

A **kingfisher** eats 60%
of its body weight in food per day.

A **grizzly bear** eats 12%
of its body weight in food per day.

FAMILY

Nothing is more important to a species than its ability to reproduce and the survival of its offspring. Life can be dangerous for newborns, which has led to many animals developing some creative solutions for looking after their young.

In some cases, the mother and father work together to ensure that their babies are given the best start in life – often keeping them safe in nests and feeding them until they're grown and ready to survive on their own.

Other animals, like wolves, form large extended families. Groups of wolves, called packs, live and hunt together, and all members of the pack benefit from a successful hunt, making teamwork important.

In this section you'll find some family arrangements that are similar to your own, and some that might seem strange. Can you imagine living in a burrow with three hundred of your siblings? Read on...

BRINGING UP BABY

Animals rear their young in many different ways. Here are some different examples.

KICK START
Koalas live alone and make incredibly protective mothers.

GRR!

Single mum

BUM DEAL
Until her baby can process the toxic eucalyptus leaves that the adults eat, a **koala** mum feeds her joey her own droppings to build up its tolerance.

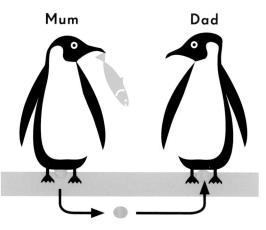

Mum   Dad

IT TAKES TWO

A female **emperor penguin** lays one egg, which the male incubates by balancing it under its stomach, on its feet. The female then searches for food. When the chick is born, Mum and Dad take turns foraging for food and caring for their young.

POLAR PARTY

Polar bears are solitary, but do gather occasionally in large groups. Baby polar bears live with their mothers for two years after birth.

Single mum

Alpha

Mates for life

Beta   Beta

Omega

LEADER OF THE PACK

Wolves live in extended family units, ruled by male and female alphas who lead the pack.

Just below the alphas of the pack are the beta wolves, who take over if anything happens to the top dogs.

At the bottom of the pack is the omega wolf, who is the last to eat and is bullied by the rest.

CUB CLUB

A **cheetah** mother has two to six cubs. She protectively rears them until they are two years old, then she leaves them to fend for themselves, heading off to start a new family elsewhere. Males are less solitary.

Single mum

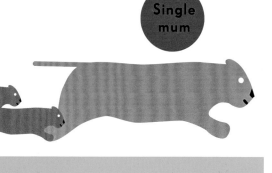

BABYSITTING

· ·

Some animals are content never to have babies themselves, but help to raise others.

As many as 220 types of birds and 120 mammals will help to rear others' young, often postponing their own chance to mate.

These animals include African wild dogs, chimpanzees, naked mole rats, lions, bee-eaters, kookaburras, Pied kingfishers, and Seychelles warblers.

MIND OUT

Meerkat pups grow up in a burrow out of danger, with babysitters taking care of them.

When they emerge into the wild, the older meerkats stand around to watch. A sentry stays on duty, looking out for danger.

QUEEN MOTHER

Naked mole rats are the first mammals ever discovered to be eusocial like bees, wasps or termites. They live in colonies of up to 300. Each group is ruled by a queen, which is the only female allowed to have babies.

The queen and two to three males reproduce. The rest are workers and are also sterile, meaning that they can't have young themselves. When the queen dies, another female takes her place.

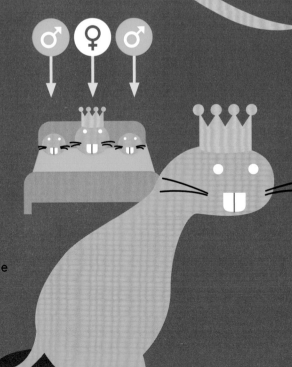

NANNY-TASTIC

Starling chicks are often brought up by a single pair of starlings, but sometimes have a helper that serves as a nanny.

READY IN THE WINGS

Florida scrub jay parents are assisted by up to six non-breeding helpers – usually their offspring from years before.

It works too! Assisted pairs successfully rear more than one and a half times as many young as those without help.

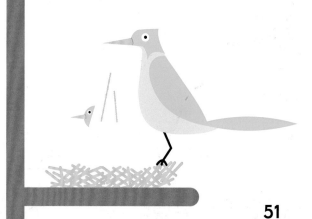

HEAD OF THE FAMILY

Different animals organise their family units in different ways.

Elephant herd
Size: 6 – 12

Mouse family
Size: 3 – 12

MOUSE HOUSE

A female **mouse** looks after her babies for around three weeks after birth, before they go their separate ways.

PINK ELEPHANTS

Elephant herds are run by the eldest female, called the matriarch. She leads her daughters and their calves until she dies. Bulls travel together in all-male pods, looking for female families to mate with.

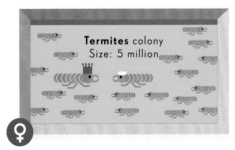

Termites colony
Size: 5 million

TREATED LIKE ROYALTY

Termite colonies are ruled by a queen. She pairs with a king and mates with him for life. They are looked after by millions of worker and soldier termites.

Lion pride
Size: around 9

PRIDE OF PLACE

Lions are the only cats to live in large family groups. One or two males rule, whilst the female lionesses do most of the hunting. When male cubs grow up they leave the pride and become nomads, searching out another to join.

POD SQUAD

Killer whales have a complex family structure, similar to elephants, with pods ruled by females. Offspring stay with their mothers all their lives. Females can live to ninety, meaning that as many as four generations can travel together.

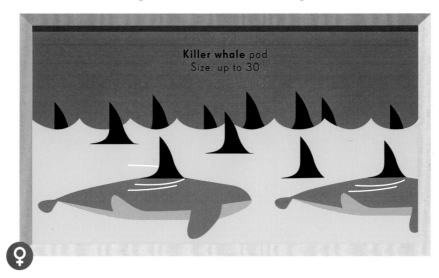

Killer whale pod
Size: up to 30

Bonobos family
Size: up to 100

HAPPY FAMILIES

Bonobos are one of the closest relatives to humans, and are very social creatures. They live in peaceful female-led family groups that change all the time as members leave to hunt for food. Different groups may sometimes meet and spend time grooming each other to be friendly.

CURIOSITIES

MIX AND MATCH

Some creatures are able to mate with other species. Their offspring are called hybrids. Here are some examples:

BEEFED UP

Beefalo are hardier than cattle and have a longer lifespan thanks to their ability to cope with harsher climates and eat a wider variety of foods. They were first found in the wild, but are now bred by humans.

American bison + Beef cattle = Beefalo

BAD CAMA

The first **cama** was born in 1998 and was bred by humans to be strong like a camel and woolly like a llama. Unfortunately, camas turned out to be rather irritable.

Camel + Llama = Cama

WILD AND WOOLLY

While some hybrids have a mixture of characteristics from both its parents, a **geep** has a mosaic of different features, with separate sheep parts that are woolly and goat parts that are hairy.

Goat + Sheep = Geep

RARE WHOLPHIN

There are very few **wholphins** in the world. Their characteristics fall midway between each parent – right down to their teeth! A false killer whale has 44 teeth, a bottlenose dolphin has 88, and a wholphin has 66!

False killer whale + Bottlenose dolphin = Wholphin

BIG FISH

Unlike the huge female **anglerfish** (which has the light-like attachment to attract prey), the male anglerfish is tiny.

TWO BECOME ONE

When the pair mate, the male burrows into her body and is eventually absorbed. The unlucky male dies in the process, but his sperm is used to fertilise the female's eggs.

1

2

55

HABITATS

An animal's habitat is its natural home or environment. Habitats vary wildly around the world, from the hot, humid rainforests to the cold, barren poles.

Climate plays a big role in shaping a given habitat; factors such as varying temperatures or limited annual rainfall determine the types of plants, and animals that can live there.

Every habitat presents its own difficulties, whether it be extreme temperatures or limited amounts of food, water or land. So each species that lives there has adapted to be uniquely in tune with its surroundings.

Humans have had a major effect on habitats around the world, building over natural landscapes and changing what grows there. Global warming is also affecting weather patterns and average temperatures, meaning that habitats are changing and animals now face different and more extreme challenges in order to survive.

Here is a look at some of the some of the world's most interesting habitats and how they are beginning to change...

JUST DESERTS

A desert is an area where very little rain falls. Most receive less than 250 millimetres/10 inches of rain per year (around ten times less than a rainforest) which allows very little vegetation to grow.

BLOWING HOT AND COLD

Deserts can be divided into two varieties: cold deserts and hot deserts.

Cold deserts are iced over for some of the year, but the frozen water cannot be absorbed by plants.

Hot deserts can hit very high temperatures in the day, which causes the water to evaporate.

The Sahara alone covers 3.5 million square miles/9 million square kilometres of the Earth.

BORN SURVIVOR

Not many animals can live in these harsh conditions, but some creatures have adapted in amazing ways to survive.

DUNE ATTUNED

Dromedary camels make up 90% of the world's camel population.

They can drink up to 35 gallons/159 litres of water in ten minutes!

Long eyelashes protect their eyes from blowing sands.

Wide feet stop them from sinking into the ground.

35 gallons

SLEEP IT OFF

Many desert animals are nocturnal. They sleep under rocks and in underground burrows during the day to keep out of the hot temperatures.

Kangaroo rats and **scorpions** are both nocturnal.

58

GRASS IS GREENER

Grasslands are areas covered mostly with grasses. They can be found on every continent other than Antarctica.

WELL-TEMPERED

Temperate grasslands can be found away from the coast. They have cold winters and warm, dry summers.

HOT TROPICS

Tropical grasslands are generally warm year-round and have a higher rainfall thanks to a wet season.

BIG OUTDOORS

Many of the world's large herbivores, such as bison, **giraffes**, **zebras** and rhinoceroses, live in grasslands.

MOVING ON

Many herbivores form migratory herds, which follow the rains and graze on the grasses through the seasons.

CUT TO THE CHASE

These herds are hunted by some of the world's biggest carnivores, such as **lions**, wolves, leopards and cheetahs.

SMALL FORTUNE

Many smaller creatures thrive in the grasslands, including **butterflies**, beetles, and mice.

POLES APART

The Arctic and Antarctic make up the polar regions. They can be found at the most northern and southern points on Earth and are its coldest habitats.

White Antarctic ice reflects more sun than it absorbs, which keeps Earth's temperature down.

ARCTIC

The Arctic is made up of islands of sea ice that drift around the North Pole.

It is iced over year-round, but the covered area expands during its ice-cold winters and shrinks during its summers (which remain at a cool temperature).

BEAR NECESSITIES

Polar bears have adapted to live in the Arctic.

A thick white coat keeps them warm and camouflaged.

Large feet stop them from sinking into the snow and make them great swimmers.

BIG BIRD

Emperor penguins are the biggest and hardiest of all the penguins. Large colonies group together annually in the Antarctic to breed.

An emperor penguin can dive up to 565 metres/1,850 feet, which is deeper than any bird.

ANTARCTIC

The Antarctic is land, but is surrounded by ice – some of it over 1 mile/1.6 kilometres thick!

Polar bears can travel up to 3,000 miles/ 4,828 kilometres in search of food.

Zzzz

CHILLED OUT

Specially adapted to its environment, an **Arctic fox**'s thick fur allows it to sleep in temperatures as cold as –45.5°C/ –50°F without causing any problems.

Its paws are well supplied with blood, which prevents them from freezing in the snow.

TUNDRA

Around the poles is the tundra – a cold, treeless area with ground which stays frozen year-round.

Mosses, lichens and shrubs can grow here, sustaining **reindeer**, Arctic hares, and lemmings, amongst other animals.

RAINFOREST

Rainforests are home to half of all the living animal and plant species in the world. Up to 80% of all insects live there, with millions more thought to still be undiscovered!

UNDER THREAT

Rainforests are among the most threatened habitats in the world – it's estimated that about half of the Earth's tropical forests have now been cut down.

WET AND WILD

Tropical rainforests are found near the equator and stay hot and humid, receiving up to 2,000 millimetres/ 78 inches of rainfall through the year.

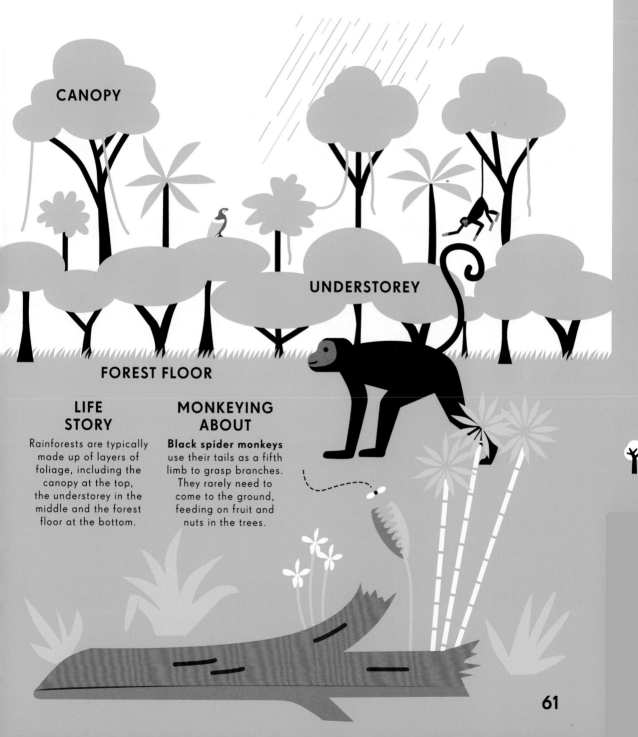

CANOPY

UNDERSTOREY

FOREST FLOOR

LIFE STORY

Rainforests are typically made up of layers of foliage, including the canopy at the top, the understorey in the middle and the forest floor at the bottom.

MONKEYING ABOUT

Black spider monkeys use their tails as a fifth limb to grasp branches. They rarely need to come to the ground, feeding on fruit and nuts in the trees.

URBAN ARRAY

Any animals that live here have to cope with unnatural sources of light, sound and food. Some have adapted very successfully, including mice, pigeons, rats, squirrels and foxes.

Urban habitats are areas where the natural landscape has been built over with human constructions.

GOING TO TOWN

Pigeons are a familiar sight in town squares around the world. They are the offspring of domestic pigeons that returned to the wild.

CITY SLICKER

There is often a higher population of **foxes** in an urban environment compared to the surrounding countryside.

It's estimated that there are around 10,000 **foxes** living in London, England.

RATTED OUT

Rats like to live near humans, as food is often found nearby. They are considered pests as they steal food, damage property and spread disease.

ROAD RAGE

60% of red **foxes** in Bristol, England, are killed by cars.

FARM FRIENDLY

Farmland – an area that has been cleared by humans to grow crops or rear animals for food – doesn't support the number of species that might live there naturally, but the fields are often bordered by hedgerows and forests where natural wildlife can be found.

BLOWN WIDE OPEN

Barn owls benefit from the wide open spaces found on farms. They are able to swoop down on mice and voles that are left exposed when they venture out in the flat fields.

HEDGED IN

Hedges are important for increasing the diversity of wildlife in an area. Records show that more than 600 plants, 1,500 insects, 65 birds, and 20 mammal species live or feed in hedgerows.

CROPPING UP

Fields of crops attract many kinds of insects, birds and rodents, who feed on them. Some farmers use pesticides to kill the insects, so that less of their crops are destroyed.

HOT TOPIC

Habitats around the world are under threat because of global warming – a rise in the temperature of the Earth's atmosphere. It is making deserts expand and get hotter, affecting weather patterns, reducing crop yields from farms, and melting ice in the polar regions.

GOOD ATMOSPHERE

The Earth is warmed by rays of heat from the sun and is surrounded by an atmosphere (a layer of gasses) that allows some of this heat to be reflected back out into space, protecting life below.

HOTTING UP

Some scientists predict that a baby born today will experience a global rise in temperature of 6.5°C/10.8°F in its lifetime.

MELT DOWN

Global warming means that ice in the polar regions is melting. Sea levels are rising because of this, leading to widespread flooding.

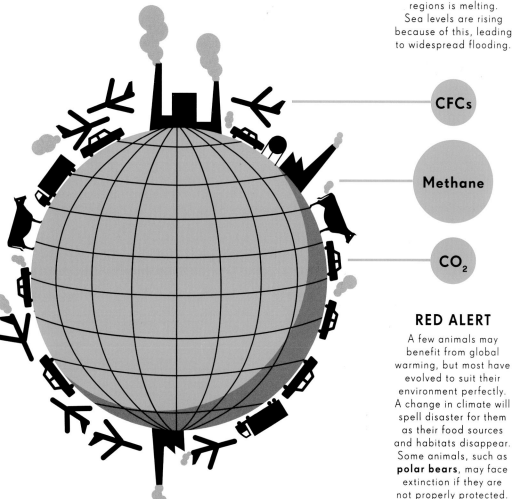

CFCs

Methane

CO_2

RED ALERT

A few animals may benefit from global warming, but most have evolved to suit their environment perfectly. A change in climate will spell disaster for them as their food sources and habitats disappear. Some animals, such as **polar bears**, may face extinction if they are not properly protected.

COOKING WITH GAS

Global warming is caused by greenhouse gasses, including carbon dioxide (CO_2), methane, and CFCs (chlorofluorocarbons).

HOT HOUSE

Having too many greenhouse gases in the Earth's atmosphere stops heat from escaping, leading to a rise in temperature.

MAN-MADE MISFORTUNE

Greenhouse gases do occur naturally, but our reliance on fossil fuels and destruction of the rainforests is speeding up global warming.

KILLERS

It's a dog-eat-dog world out in the wild, and many animals have to fight to survive.

Hunger is one of the main reasons that an animal will kill. Predators need to use deadly weapons – such as claws, teeth and venom – to become successful hunters.

In response, hunted animals have had to develop some pretty tough defence mechanisms, and whilst they may not go looking for a fight, a tussle with some of these naturally docile creatures can have fatal consequences.

Some of nature's most savage battles can be fought between two animals of the same species. Fighting for mating rights with a female ensures the strongest animal's genes will be passed on, and with such high odds, these battles can be ferociously fought. Staking claim to the best patch of land can also be a matter of life or death to an animal, leading to fierce turf wars.

Take a look at some of the deadliest, strangest, and most underrated natural born killers out there...

FIGHT CLUB

Many animals are forced to fight to ensure their survival. Here are some of the reasons why they turn to violence.

NO TRESPASSING

An animal's territory – the area of land it lives in – is key to its survival, as this is where it finds food, rears young and keeps out of danger. It is so important that many animals will kill each other for rights to the best plot.

TURF WAR

Gangs of **monkeys** and chimpanzees will wage war on competing tribes to take over their territories.

The defending monkeys will scream and bark to scare off the attackers, rattling branches and throwing sticks and faeces.

BIG BUCKS

Male **rabbits** are very territorial and will fight to the death to protect their land.

CROCODILE SHOO

Hippos will often attack – and sometimes kill – crocodiles for the best spot in the swamp.

FIGHTING CHANCE

In nature, females want to make sure that they pass on the strongest genes to their offspring to give them the best chance of survival. This can make mating a dangerous business for the males, who sometimes have to fight to impress the females.

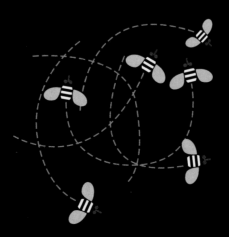

KILLER BEES

Male Dawson's bees are one of the largest and most aggressive species of bee. They engage in a massive fighting frenzy to win the right to mate with a female. The fighting leaves most of the males (as well as many females) dead.

KILLER INSTINCT

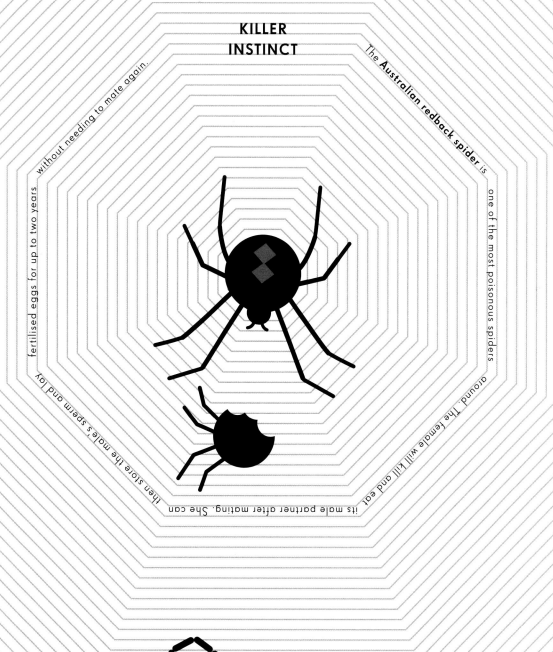

The **Australian redback spider** is one of the most poisonous spiders around. The female will kill and eat its male partner after mating. She can then store the male's sperm and lay fertilised eggs for up to two years without needing to mate again.

DEADLY EMBRACE

Female **scorpions** often kill the males once they have mated, injecting them with a series of lethal stings before eating them.

ROMANCE IS DEAD

In nature, some females have no more need for their partner once they have used them to mate, and simply kill them afterwards. Even in death, this can give the male an advantage over his rivals: once the female has eaten his body, she is unlikely to go looking for another mate, meaning his genes are the ones that will be passed on in the eggs the female lays.

67

KILLING MACHINE

Lots of animals in nature are built to kill – having to hunt for their food to stay safe from starvation.

SILENT BUT DEADLY
Many are famed for their strength, speed or deadly weaponry, but here are some of the most underrated predators out there.

NAUGHTY KITTY
Domestic **cats** kill up to 3.7 billion birds and over 20 billion small mammals a year in the United States.

DEVILISH GRIN

The Tasmanian devil is the size of a small dog and is the world's largest carnivorous marsupial. It has the strongest bite in comparison to its weight of any living animal.

BADGER TO DEATH

The **honey badger** has sharp teeth, strong jaws and long claws, which it uses to kill and eat venomous snakes, raid beehives for their honey and even steal food from young lions!

TONGUE LASHING

Chameleons have stereoscopic eyes and 360-degree vision, making it hard for prey to go undetected. With a tongue three times the length of its body, it can hit prey in 30 thousandths of a second.

SELF DEFENCE

Many animals have developed bizarre – and sometimes deadly – ways to defend themselves from predators.

COOL AS A CUCUMBER

The **sea cucumber** can turn itself inside out, shooting its intestines out of its body to entangle predators.

SLIPPERY CHARACTER

The **hagfish** oozes a toxic slime when under attack, helping it to squirm out of danger.

KEPT ON ITS TOES

The **hairy frog** breaks the bones in its toes to produce 'claws'. The bones puncture through the skin on its feet to be used as defensive weapons.

EYE OPENER

The **horned lizard** can squirt foul-tasting blood from the corners of its eyes to scare off attackers. The jets of blood can travel up to 1.5 metres/5 feet.

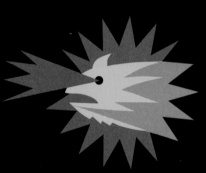

SHAKE, RATTLE AND ROLL

The **crested porcupine** will rattle its tail quills as a threat, stabbing any attacker as a final resort – sometimes fatally.

GETTING ANTSY

The **Malaysian soldier ant** has glands full of poison inside its body. When it senses a threat, it explodes, spraying poison to protect its colony.

INSECTICIDE

The **bombardier beetle** sprays a mixture of boiling toxic chemicals from its abdomen – fatal to other insects – which makes a 'pop!' sound as it is released.

REEK OF DEATH

The **opossum** 'plays dead' by slipping into a coma when it is attacked, foaming at the mouth and releasing a green liquid from its backside that smells like a corpse.

READY TO ROLL

The **pangolin** is covered in scales and rolls into a very tight ball – sometimes down a hill – to escape its enemies.

HEADS OR TAILS

If a **dormouse** is caught by the tail, it can make its tail drop off, helping it to escape.

STICKY SITUATION

The **fulmar** chick launches a sticky orange goo at attackers. This substance glues other birds' feathers together so that they can't fly or swim in water.

STAB IN THE BACK

The male **platypus** stabs enemies with its ankle spur, injecting them with a powerful poison.

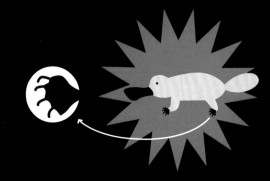

MAN'S BEST FRIEND

Ever since the last ice age, humans have lived and worked with dogs. Today's modern domesticated dogs have evolved from wolves, which were used by early humans for hunting, protection and pulling sledges. The special bond that was forged all those thousands of years ago has earned dogs the title 'man's best friend'.

Because of their good temperament and high intelligence, dogs make excellent pets. However, with their agility, strength, and especially their excellent sense of smell, dogs can be useful even in today's technological world, coming to the rescue with their specialised abilities!

Over time, humans have bred many varieties of dogs. Some are prized for their good looks, and others are bred and trained to perform certain jobs, such as herding sheep, sniffing out trouble, or guiding the blind.

Read on to find out why dogs are still man's best friend today...

WORK LIKE A DOG

Dogs aren't just great pets.
Many breeds work for humans –
sometimes even saving lives.

TO THE RESCUE
Herding dogs make
good mountain rescue
animals and are accustomed
to working with humans.

SNOWED UNDER
Humans lose around 40,000
scented skin cells per hour, which
trained avalanche dogs sniff out
by burying their heads in the snow.
If the smell gets stronger, they
keep digging. If it gets weaker,
they start digging nearby until it's
stronger again.

TOP DOG

A team of twenty
people searching
for an avalanche
victim expect to
cover 1 hectare/
2.5 acres of land
in four hours.
A mountain rescue
dog can do it in
30 minutes – an
eighth of the time.

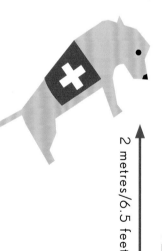

DIG DEEP
Most dogs can find people
buried under about
2 metres/6.5 feet of snow.

One man in the United States
was found under 10 metres/
33 feet of snow.

Another man in Austria was rescued
beneath 12 metres/39 feet of snow.

2 metres/6.5 feet

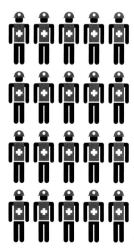

WHIFF OF TROUBLE

German police collected scents from political activists to enable their dogs to trace people they believed might try to violently disrupt the 2007 G8 summit.

CARRIED AWAY

The most famous Saint Bernard was named Barry. He was bred at the Great Saint Bernard Hospice in Switzerland. He rescued forty people, most famously a young boy whom he discovered, manoeuvred onto his back, and carried to safety.

Saint Bernards aren't often used as rescue dogs, and contrary to legend they never have small kegs of whisky tied around their necks.

TIME MATTERS

90% of people buried in avalanches survive if they are recovered in the first 15 minutes.

Only 30% survive after 30 minutes.

Just 3% live if buried for more than 2 hours.

DEATH SCENT

When emergency services are searching for a body rather than a living person they need a different kind of dog: a cadaver dog, trained to detect rotting flesh.

SEEING DOGS

Guide dogs help partially-sighted and blind people, by safely navigating them about.

SMELL A RAT

Dogs are used to sniff other things too, such as...

cash   **explosives**   **drugs**

DOG BONES

Dogs come in all shapes and sizes, but they share the same body parts.

BRAIN

Dogs' brains have evolved to become smaller since humans domesticated them. A four-month-old wolf pup in the wild has a bigger brain than a fully grown dog.

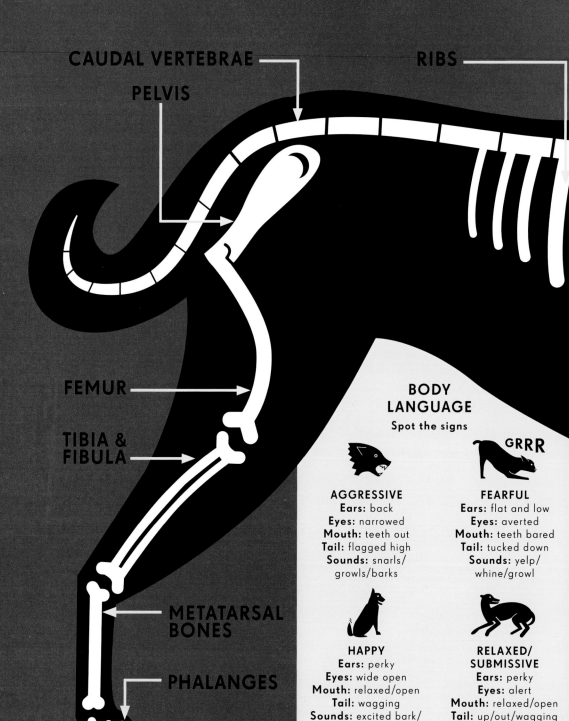

CAUDAL VERTEBRAE

RIBS

PELVIS

FEMUR

TIBIA & FIBULA

METATARSAL BONES

PHALANGES

BODY LANGUAGE
Spot the signs

AGGRESSIVE
Ears: back
Eyes: narrowed
Mouth: teeth out
Tail: flagged high
Sounds: snarls/ growls/barks

GRRR

FEARFUL
Ears: flat and low
Eyes: averted
Mouth: teeth bared
Tail: tucked down
Sounds: yelp/ whine/growl

HAPPY
Ears: perky
Eyes: wide open
Mouth: relaxed/open
Tail: wagging
Sounds: excited bark/ playful growl

RELAXED/ SUBMISSIVE
Ears: perky
Eyes: alert
Mouth: relaxed/open
Tail: up/out/wagging
Sounds: whimper/yap

NASAL CAVITY

OESOPHAGUS

TRACHEA

SCAPULA

HAPPY WAGGING
Usually, dogs wag their tails to express happiness. However...

when dogs feel positive about someone, their tails wag more to the right...

and when they have negative feelings, their tail wagging is biased to the left.

LUNGS

HEART

HUMERUS

RADIUS & ULNA

METACARPAL BONES

PHALANGES

BEST IN SHOW

Many dogs were originally bred to work for humans – although they are often more likely to be pets now. See what they were designed for in the first place.

COLLIE
Herding and working.

JACK RUSSELL
Accompanying fox hunts.

DOBERMAN PINSCHER
Protecting humans – often used as guard and police dogs.

LABRADOR RETRIEVER
Helping fishermen retrieve their catch from the water by pulling nets in.

BOXER
Descendant of Tibetan fighting dogs and German hunting dogs.

KUVASZ
Owned and bred only by aristocracy for hunting and guarding.

WOOF!

TERRIER
Catching rats, rabbits and foxes.

BLACK RUSSIAN TERRIER
Guard dogs
for the Soviet army.

ANATOLIAN SHEPHERD
Guarding sheep and goats.

CHIHUAHUA
Bred as pets in
ancient Mexico.

GREAT DANE
Guarding – bred in
ancient Egypt for ferocity.

STANDARD POODLE
Hunting and retrieving waterfowl.

SAMOYED
Pulling sledges across the snow and ice, usually in a team.

BIG PICTURE PRESS
www.bigpicturepress.net

First published in the UK and Australia in 2014 by Big Picture Press,
part of the Bonnier Publishing Group,
The Plaza, 535 King's Road, London, SW10 0SZ
www.bonnierpublishing.com

ISBN 978-1-84877-654-8

Printed in China

This book was typeset in Super Grotesk
The illustrations were created digitally

Designed by Joe Hales
Edited by Jenny Broom
With thanks to Ami Sedghi

· ·

Nicholas Blechman is an internationally recognised illustrator, designer and art director based in New York. His award-winning illustrations have appeared in *GQ*, *Travel + Leisure*, *Wired*, and the *New Yorker*. He is currently the Art Director of the *New York Times Book Review* and has taught design at School of Visual Arts and illustration at the Maryland Institute College of Art.

Simon Rogers edited and created guardian.co.uk/data, probably the world's most popular data journalism website and online data resource. Publishing hundreds of raw data sets, it encourages its users to visualise and analyse them. He has previously worked at Twitter in San Francisco as the organisation's first Data Editor.